DAVID AND BATHSHEBA

CONSEQUENCES OF ADULTERY

LESLIE M. JOHN

DAVID AND BATHSHEBA

CONSEQUENCES OF ADULTERY

LESLIE M. JOHN

My mission is to proclaim the good news of our Lord Jesus Christ as revealed to me through Holy

Bible and from various teachers, preachers, and commentators.

This is my voluntary service to God in the name of His only begotten Son Lord Jesus Christ. I share the truth of knowledge of God with others with good intention of bringing them to the knowledge of the living God, the God of Abraham, the God of Isaac, the God of Jacob, and the Father of our Lord Jesus Christ.

My mission is to proclaim the Gospel of Lord Jesus Christ and not converting forcibly anyone to Christianity. One may accept or reject any or part of my writings/teachings.

All Scriptures are taken from KJV from open domain

ISBN-13: 978-0989028325

ISBN-10: 0989028321

DAVID AND BATHSHEBA

TABLE OF CONTENTS

DAVID AND BATHSHEBA................................1

CONSEQUENCES OF ADULTERY...........................1

INTRODUCTION 8

CHAPTER 1 NATHAN ADMONISHES DAVID........13

CHAPTER 2 UNDESIRED PREGNANCY OF
BATHSHEBA 17

CONSPIRACY AGAINST URIAH...........18

PURIFICATION.........................20

CHAPTER 3 WHO WERE HITTITES?.........29

CHAPTER 4 DAVID REPENTS OF HIS SIN...............32

CHAPTER 5 DAVID'S FIRST SON DIES....................35

CHAPTER 6 AMNON RAPES HIS SISTER TAMAR.38

SIN LEAVES BEHIND ITS SCARS!...........38

CHAPTER 7 ABSALOM FLEES....................45

CHAPETR 8 DAVID FLEES...........................53

CHAPTER 9 ADONIJAH AND SOLOMON............57

CHAPPTER 10 DAVID THANKS GOD...............61

CHAPTER 11 DAVID HONORED GOD..................65

CHAPTER 12 MEPHIBOSHETH...............69

CHAPTER 13 SECURITY OF BELIEVER IN CHRIST.72

THE LOVE OF GOD 76

GOD HAS CHOSEN US...............78

THE SEVERITY OF JUDGMENT.............81

CHAPTER 14 REDEEMED FROM BONDAGE OF SIN
...............83

CHAPTER 15 THOUSAND YEAR REIGN 91

CHAPTER 16 DAVID'S THRONE ESTABLISHED FOR EVER................96

CHAPTER 17 JERUSALEM WILL BE CALLED BY A NEW NAME................100

CHAPTER 18 MESSAGE OF CROSS............105

HIS ONLY BEGOTTEN SON 109

SALVATION IS FREE OF COST 109

CHAPTER 19 INVITATION TO SALVATION..........111

GOD IS A SPIRIT...............111

HAS ANYONE SEEN GOD? 113

JESUS WAS BORN AS MAN 113

JESUS WAS FULLY DIVINE AND FULLY HUMAN
....116

MOSES DESIRED TO SEE GOD...........119

HOW DID GOD SPEAK TO MAN? 121

GOD SPOKE IN DIFFERENT WAYS..............124

GOD SPOKE BY HIS SON 127

INTRODUCTION

"And when he had removed him, he raised up unto them David to be their king; to whom also he gave testimony, and said, I have found David the son of Jesse, a man after mine own heart, which shall fulfill all my will". (Acts 13:22)

It was indeed grace of God that David was saved from his atrocious sin and yet he had to pay for the sin he had committed. When we read how David committed adultery with Bathsheba and killed her husband it is beyond man's imagination that God would forgive him of his sin.

David was called a man of wars and won many battles with the help of God an yet when he numbered his army he faced defeat. He desired to build a temple for God but God said he cannot build a temple for Him because his hands are full of blood. However, God blessed his son Solomon and allowed him to build temple for Him.

God promised that the throne of David through Solomon will be established for ever and ever. The Lord is compassionate and slow to anger. Lord

Jesus is born in the lineage of David and loved to call Himself as the son of David.

"The book of the generation of Jesus Christ, the son of David, the son of Abraham". (Matthew 1:1)

"Kiss the Son, lest he be angry, and ye perish from the way, when his wrath is kindled but a little. Blessed are all they that put their trust in him". (Psalms 2:12)

Psalmist having said in Psalms chapter 1 that the godly should not have company with ungodly now wonders as to why the ungodly and sinners imagine vain things such as to ridicule the living God and work against the children of the living God.

Those who are saved in the precious blood of Jesus Christ are the Children of God.

Apostle Paul writes: "For ye are all the children of God by faith in Christ Jesus" (Galatians 3:26).

Mighty kings, princes, wise men, and dictators have come and gone but none lived and ruled like our living God who is eternal. He rules the earth; he is there everywhere. Man's thoughts are not

God's thoughts. His ways are higher than ours. He is mightier than anybody. When man takes refuge in his own strength and wisdom the Lord will have him in derision.

The Father says He has set Jesus upon the holy hill of Zion. This is a prophecy and it is about the thousand year peaceful reign of our Lord Jesus Christ from the throne of David. The Father promises that the uttermost parts will be given to The Son for his possession.

Jesus is the Son of God and he shall break the mighty men with iron rod and he breaks them as the rod strikes a potter's vessel. There were mighty men such as Sihon, king of Amoties, Og, the king of Bashaan, and Goliath in Philistine army but none prevailed against God and the children of Israel.

Sihon, king of the Amorites, opposed and tried to prevent in vain the Israelites to pass through his territory. The result was that he was defeated and Israelites not only took possession of his cities but they had their way through the land of Amorites. (Numbers 21:21-24)

Og, the king of Bashan, who was ruler over sixty cities, went out against Israelites but God assured Moses of his help and he defeated Og, the king of Bashan and took possession of his land. (Numbers 21:33-35)

There was a mighty man in Philistine army and he was Goliath. But David, a shepherd boy, son of Jessy, with the help of the Almighty God defeated Goliath miraculously when he slang one smooth stone from his sling that struck on his forehead and Goliath fell face down on the ground. David pulled out Goliath's sword from his sheath and killed him.

There were other mighty men like Alexander the great, Napoleon, Hitler, etc. Some of them were great and some of them were terror to others; but all of them died.

Many dictators who stood strong defiantly in the recent past fell down and lost their positions. Above all one that rules is our living God and His only begotten Son, Lord Jesus Christ is our Savior. Are we greater than these mighty men? If not, then let us depend upon the living God and worship him.

Psalmist points to antitype in Psalm Chapter 2 and exhorts, therefore, to serve Jesus with fear and rejoice. There is an interesting phrase used and it is "Kiss the Son".

It is not an advice for us to kiss our sons but it is an exhortation to worship the Son of God, Lord Jesus Christ. It is very good that we kiss our sons, but here in this context it is not an exhortation to kiss our sons but it is an exhortation to worship the Son of God, Lord Jesus Christ.

There is warning that if we do not worship the Son of God he would be angry and we may perish from the way. Psalmist says that those who put their trust in the Lord will be blessed.

Let us say as the children of Israel said when Joshua challenged them with a question as to whom they prefer to serve; whether it is idols or the living God! They all answered and said without any hesitation: "We will serve the LORD".

"And the people said unto Joshua, Nay; but we will serve the LORD". (Joshua 24:21)

CHAPTER 1
NATHAN ADMONISHES DAVID

God sent Nathan, the Prophet of God, to King David. The Prophet narrated a story to King David, according to the word of the LORD, and he asked the King what the resolution of the problem should be.

The story goes on that there were two men in a city; one rich and other poor. The rich man's wealth was in his possession of many flocks and herds while the poor man had nothing except a little ewe lamb.

The poor man had bought that little ewe lamb and nourished it up with great love. The ewe lamb grew up in the house of the poor man and played with his children. It also ate the poor man's food, drank from poor man's cup, and lay in his bosom and was like his daughter.

It so happened that the rich man had a traveler visiting him. What usually happens in a home is that the master of the house makes arrangements for the visitor from his own possessions and treats him but here the rich man did something strange and unpleasant deed. He grabbed by force the poor man's ewe lamb that the poor man so loved as his daughter and the rich man killed the lamb and made a feast of it for the visitor.

Is it not atrocious for a man to take another man's loved pet and kill it and make a feast of it for his guest?

If he were a loving one he should offer food from his barns but the rich man took the loved pet of poor man, killed it and offered its meat as food for the traveler visiting him. It is like robbing Peter to pay Paul. And, what an unfair deal it was that the rich man robbing the pet of the poor man to treat rich man's guest!

King David heard this story and he burst out in anger and pronounced that the rich man be penalized to death and restore to the poor man fourfold for his unlawful and ungracious act in killing poor man's ewe lamb and had no pity on either the poor man or the ewe lamb.

Guess what! Nathan the prophet of God said to King David that he was that rich man who robbed the poor man's ewe lamb to feed his guest.

The LORD spoke to King David through Nathan the prophet that He anointed David as the King over Israel and delivered him out of the hand of Saul, and the LORD not only gave his master's house to him and his master's wives into his bosom He also gave the 'House of Israel' and the 'House of Judah'.

The LORD also said that if David thought the gifts from God were short of his expectation King David should have asked of the LORD for more and the LORD would have given him surely his desires. But it was not so. King David preferred to rob poor man's possession and sacrifice it for the sake of fulfilling his appetite. The possession of the poor man was not an ordinary ewe lamb as described in the story nor the appetite of King David was a meal, but the poor man's loved possession was his wife and the appetite of King David was his lust and adultery.

When Nathan the prophet told the deeds that King David did he pronounced death of the man who committed such horrendous act and to return four fold of what he robbed. And, when the story was attributed to his acts it was unbearable for King David. He realized the adultery with Bathsheba and killing Uriah, Bathsheba's husband.

CHAPTER 2
UNDESIRED PREGNANCY OF
BATHSHEBA

Conspiracy against Uriah the husband of
Bathsheba upon whom David the king had cast
his eyes and lusted after her and subdued her in
his power as king to commit adultery produced an
undesired pregnancy that caused mental agony
for him. He had to commit more sins to hide the
first sin.

King David committed adultery with Bathsheba,
the wife of Uriah, the Hittite and after her days of
purification were over she returned to her home.
Bathsheba conceived and sent word to King David
that she was with child.

Not losing much time David made arrangements
to see that Uriah, her husband returned to David
from the battle field. David summoned Uriah from
the battle field and when Uriah came and stood
before him he inquired of Joab and the people
and how the war prospered.

David was very in quick in scheming that Uriah would go his home and sleep at his home with his wife who was pregnant. His scheme failed because God intended otherwise.

Uriah, not knowing what happened in his absence, left the presence of David but honest as he was he slept at the door of the king's house.

When David came to know that Uriah did not go home and sleep at his home but he slept at King's door he inquired of Uriah as to why he did not go his home and sleep at his home.

Uriah replied that The ark, and Israel, and Judah abide in tents, and Joab his lord and the servants of Joab are in the open fields fighting the battle. Uriah wondered before King David as to how inn such circumstances he could go home and sleep with his wife. He swore by the name of king and said he would not resort to doing such disloyal deed.

CONSPIRACY AGAINST URIAH

King David said to Uriah to stay there that day also and also the next and then he could go. Uriah stayed back in Jerusalem that day and the morrow and at the invitation of the King he ate with the king and drank with him.

When Uriah was drunk David wrote a letter to Joab and sent it to him by the hand of Uriah. The letter was in the hands of Uriah but he did not know the contents of the letter.

The letter was written by the king. Uriah carried the letter containing the order to Joab that he be placed in the front hot spot in the battle to be killed. Uriah carried his death order in his own hand.

The king defiled chastity of Uriah's wife Bathsheba and he ordered that Uriah should be placed in the hot spot in the battle field in order that he could be killed.

What an atrocious act! Uriah was honest to the extent that he did not go his home to sleep with his wife even after returning from the battle field for a period of time when king summoned him and gave the opportunity to be with his wife. The king, of course, had conspired that the child in the womb of Bathsheba is called Uriah's child but when that idea failed he got Uriah killed in the battle field.

The letter from king David contained clear instructions to Joab that Uriah be set in the forefront of the hottest battle and withdraw from him to see that he was left without much support and be smitten and die. Joab obeyed the instructions from King David and assigned Uriah a place where he could face valiant men in the battle.

As per the scheme of king David Uriah was killed in the battle. Some interesting events happened in the meanwhile. The men of city went out and fought with Joab and Joab escaped death but the servants of David were killed.

PURIFICATION

After her purification from her uncleanness she returned to her home. Interesting! What is purification and what did Bathsheba do for her purification?

When Bathsheba was in the house of David she was clean of her menstrual period and her pregnancy was surely that from David.

According to Mosaic Law if a woman conceives seed and bears a male child then she shall be unclean seven days and on the eighth day the flesh of the foreskin of the child be circumcised. She shall continue to be in the blood of her purification for thirty three days more from the seventh day of her uncleanness. That is to say that the woman can return to her home only after forty days.

However, if she bears a female child she shall be unclean for two weeks in separation and continue to be as 'unclean' for sixty six days.

After her purification days are over for a son or for a daughter she should bring a lamb of the first year for a burnt offering, a young pigeon or turtledove, for a sin offering to the door of the tabernacle of the congregation and give it to the priest, who shall offer it before the LORD to make an atonement for her.

After offering the sacrifice the woman shall be cleansed of her blood. If the woman is poor she could bring two turtledoves or two pigeons instead of lamb and a pigeon or turtledove, one for the burnt offering and another for sin offering.

The priest shall make atonement for her and she shall be clean. (Ref. Leviticus 12:1-8)

When Jesus was born wise men from the east of Jerusalem inquired as to where Jesus was born. Herod the king was greatly troubled and said to the wise men that after finding Jesus and worshipping Him they could come and inform him in order that he may go and worship them.

However, after the wise men worshipped Jesus and according to the word of the Lord they went another way and Herod raged in anger and ordered killing of all the babies two years and younger.

The angel of the Lord appeared to Joseph in a dream and said to him to take the young child and his mother and flee to Egypt and be there until he appears to him again and give instructions. According the word of the Lord Joseph took the child and his mother by night and departed to Egypt (Ref. Matthew 2:13-14)

There were prophesies fulfilled here. One was the prophesy of Jeremiah said in 31:15

"Thus saith the LORD; A voice was heard in Ramah, lamentation, and bitter weeping; Rahel weeping for her children refused to be comforted for her children, because they were not". (Jeremiah 31:15)

The second was in Hosea 11:1

"When Israel was a child, then I loved him, and called my son out of Egypt". (Hosea 11:1)

After Herod was dead the angel of the Lord appeared to Joseph and said to him to take Mary and the child and go to Israel from Egypt. Luke's record of events during that period delves us to know more of purification.

The mother of Jesus offered two turtle doves after her purification days were over according to the Law of Moses. This shows that Jesus had a natural birth as human from Virgin Mary conceived of the Holy Ghost. Thus Jesus was fully divine and fully man when He was on this earth.

Mary needed to do the ritual according to the Law of Moses and offer burnt offering. After eight days were over and when it was time to circumcise the child she was courageous to offer the sacrifice even in the midst of the threats of Herod killing the first born. She was virgin virtuous yet she needed a Savior just as any human being on this earth.

Magi worshipped Jesus and not His mother. The worship belongs to Lord Jesus Christ who is the Savior and the mother of Jesus was virtuous and found grace in the sight of the Lord but she cannot take glory of the Lord.

"And when eight days were accomplished for the circumcising of the child, his name was called JESUS, which was so named of the angel before he was conceived in the womb. And when the days of her purification according to the Law of Moses were accomplished, they brought him to Jerusalem, to present him to the Lord; (As it is written in the law of the Lord, Every male that openeth the womb shall be called holy to the Lord ;) And to offer a sacrifice according to that which is said in the law of the Lord, A pair of turtledoves, or two young pigeons" (Luke 2:21-24)

Earlier when Elisabeth saw Mary she said "Blessed art thou among women..." and Mary replied... "My soul doth magnify the Lord, And my spirit hath rejoiced in God my Saviour". Mary knew from the word of the angel who said to her that Jesus, a savior will be born from her womb.

"And, behold, thou shalt conceive in thy womb, and bring forth a son, and shalt call his name JESUS". (Luke 1:31)

And it came to pass, that, when Elisabeth heard the salutation of Mary, the babe leaped in her womb; and Elisabeth was filled with the Holy Ghost: And she spake out with a loud voice, and said, Blessed art thou among women, and blessed is the fruit of thy womb. And whence is this to me, that the mother of my Lord should come to me? For, lo, as soon as the voice of thy salutation sounded in mine ears, the babe leaped in my womb for joy. And blessed is she that believed: for there shall be a performance of those things which were told her from the Lord. And Mary said, My soul doth magnify the Lord, And my spirit hath rejoiced in God my Saviour. (Luke 1:41-47)

Until the day Lord Jesus Christ ascended into heaven to be seated at the right hand of the

Majesty. Jesus showed He was alive with infallible proofs and was seen forty days.

Jesus and His disciples assembled and He spoke to His disciples of kingdom of God and said to them they should not depart from Jerusalem until Holy Spirit came upon them.

He said to them that they will receive power after the Holy Spirit came upon them and they shall be witnesses both in Jerusalem, and in all Judea, and in Samaria and unto uttermost part of the earth. Then they returned to Jerusalem from the mount Olivet a Sabbath day's journey and went to an upper room where eleven disciples gathered along with about one hundred and twenty people.

In that gathering Mary the mother of Jesus and other women were also there and they all continued with one accord in prayer and supplication.

"These all continued with one accord in prayer and supplication, with the women, and Mary the mother of Jesus, and with his brethren" (Acts 1:14)

The savior of this world Lord Jesus Christ relinquished His glory with the Father in heaven and took the form of a slave and was born in the likeness of man in order to bear our sins upon Himself and die for us and He was obedient even unto the death on the cross. (Ref: Philippians 2:7-11)

All those who accept Lord Jesus Christ as their savior and confess their sins to Him will receive salvation free of cost.

No amount of good works will save and salvation is obtainable with silver or gold. If Mary the mother of Lord Jesus Christ needed a savior, then we all need a savior and Bible says there is salvation under heaven except through Lord Jesus Christ.

"Forasmuch as ye know that ye were not redeemed with corruptible things, as silver and gold, from your vain conversation received by tradition from your fathers; But with the precious blood of Christ, as of a lamb without blemish and without spot" (1 Peter 1:18-19)

Jesus became poor for our sake and His earthly parents had no more than a pair of turtledoves to offer as burnt offering.

"For ye know the grace of our Lord Jesus Christ, that, though he was rich, yet for your sakes he became poor, that ye through his poverty might be rich". (2 Corinthians 8:9)

"For if there be first a willing mind, it is accepted according to that a man hath, and not according to that he hath not". (2 Corinthians 8:12)

CHAPTER 3
WHO WERE HITTITES?

Bathsheba was a beautiful young wife of Uriah the Hittite. Hittite!

When the LORD made a covenant with Abram saying unto his seed the LORD gave the land from the river of Egypt unto the great river, the river Euphrates, He also said that He will give the Kenites, Kenizzites, Kadmonites, Hittites, Perizzites, Rephaims, Amorites, Canaanites, Girgashites and Jebusites. (Ref: Genesis 15:18-21)

Abraham's grandson Jacob was renamed by God as Israel and the children of Israel were under the bondage of slavery under Pharaoh in Egypt.

They cried unto the LORD and the LORD delivered them out of the hand of Egyptians and promised them the land flowing with milk and honey. The LORD delivered them from Canaanites, Hittites, Amorites, Perizzites, Hivites, and Jebusites.

Abraham while choosing a wife for his son Isaac said to the eldest servant of his house to swear by the LORD, the God of heaven, the God of the earth that he shall not take a wife unto Isaac from the daughters of Canaanites (Cf. Genesis 24:2-3) Rebekah was from the lineage of Shem from whose lineage was Abraham and Sarah also were. Rebekah was sister of Laban who had two daughters, Leah and Rachel, who became wives of Jacob. Thus God's purpose was to keep the blessed generation aloof from others.

While dealing with Christians and unbelievers Apostle Paul writes:

"Be ye not unequally yoked together with unbelievers: for what fellowship hath righteousness with unrighteousness? and what communion hath light with darkness?" (2 Corinthians 6:14)

Hittites are believed to have come from the lineage of Heth.

"And Canaan begat Sidon his firstborn, and Heth" (Genesis 10:15) and Canaan from Ham whom Noah cursed for his abomination. And he said, Cursed be Canaan; a servant of servants shall he be unto his brethren". (Genesis 9:25)

God promised the land flowing with milk and honey to the children of Israel and said to them to utterly destroy Hittites, Amorites, Canaanites, Perizzites, Hivites, and Jebusites (Ref: Deuteronomy 20:17)

CHAPTER 4
DAVID REPENTS OF HIS SIN

David was a man of wars and God was with him. However, on one occasion when David yielded to Satan's temptation and numbered Israel he had to seek atonement for his sin.

Satan had David yield to his temptation and stand in his pride to number Israel and look upon his own strength.

All the days of his life God helped him win the wars with small number in his army. If we recall David's victory over Goliath it can be seen that he brought down the proud and hefty Philistine with just one smooth stone out of the five that he has collected from the brook.

He collected five stones in a shepherd's bag that he had and swung his sling with just one stone in it and brought down the Philistine onto the ground. Then, David ran and stood upon Goliath and drew the sword from Goliath's sheath and killed him. (1 Samuel 17:40 and 51)

Lord Jesus Christ said "But when a stronger than he shall come upon him, and overcome him, he taketh from him all his armour wherein he trusted, and divideth his spoils". (Luke 11:22)

"And Satan stood up against Israel, and provoked David to number Israel" (1 Chronicles 21:1)

In spite of Joab's efforts to try to prevent David to trespass against God's desires and against Israel, David's orders prevailed and Joab numbered the Israel. God was angry at David and his actions in numbering Israel.

God sent an angel to destroy Jerusalem and as the angel of the LORD was destroying Jerusalem, David repented of the evil he did and said to the angel to stop destroying.

He saw the angel of the Lord standing between the earth and heaven having a drawn sword in his hand stretched out over Jerusalem. David and elders of Israel wore sack clothes and fell upon their faces.

David accepted that he sinned against God and prayed that he may be punished but not his people because it was he who sinned against the Lord. The LORD saw that David repented of his sin.

David built an altar in the threshingfloor of Ornan the Jebusite, according to the desire of the LORD as ordered by the angel of the LORD through Gad who conveyed the words of the angel of the LORD to him.

David paid full price of the land, the oxen, and the threshing instruments for wood and also for wheat that was needed for the meat offering. David refused to take all these free of cost. He paid Ornan, six hundred shekels of gold by weight.

David built there an altar unto the LORD. The LORD, then asked the angel of the LORD to put his sword in his sheath. When David saw that the LORD answered his prayer in the threshing floor of Ornan, he sacrificed there. (1 Chronicles 21:28)

There is reconciliation when we pray and accept before God our sins. God forgives us our iniquity.

CHAPTER 5
DAVID'S FIRST SON DIES

Nathan the prophet said to David that he gave great occasion to the enemies of Jehovah to blaspheme the LORD because of the son born to Bathsheba as a consequence of his lust and adultery with her. The prophet prophesied that the child born to Bathsheba from David will surely die.

Nathan left to his house after admonishing King David and the LORD struck the child born to Uriah's wife Bathsheba unto David.

The child fell very sick and the LORD did not pay attention to David's prayer for the child. David fasted and lay all night upon the earth insomuch that the elders of his house went to him and helped him to rise from the earth.

On the seventh day the child died. The servants of David were sore afraid to talk to him because he did not listen to their plea earlier when the child was sick and wondered how he would listen to their plea for cease from fasting. The servant felt that he would harm himself more than how did to himself in fasting and praying for the child.

As the servants spoke to one another about the dead child David heard their whispering and perceived that the child died. He inquired of the servants if the child was dead and they answered him that the child died.

Contrary to their thinking David rose from the earth, washed and anointed himself and changed his garments and went into the house of the LORD and worshiped Him. After worshipping the LORD he went home and ate sumptuously.

Indeed the servants were surprised that David fasted and prayed for the child but when his prayer was rejected by the LORD he rose and had his apparel put on him, anointed himself after washing himself, went and worshipped God and thereafter ate food to his satisfaction. They inquired David of his behavior and he responded saying

"... While the child was yet alive, I fasted and wept: for I said, Who can tell whether GOD will be gracious to me, that the child may live? But now he is dead, wherefore should I fast? can I bring him back again? I shall go to him, but he shall not return to me"

David married Bathsheba and she became his wife and he went into unto her and lay with her and she bore a son for him. David called his name as "Solomon" and the LORD loved Solomon. (cr. 2 Samuel 12:14-31)

CHAPTER 6
AMNON RAPES HIS SISTER TAMAR

SIN LEAVES BEHIND ITS SCARS!

Nathan the prophet narrated a story that appeared to be fiction for King David and he said to Nathan that the offender should be greatly punished.

Not losing much time Nathan the prophet said to David that he was the one who did evil in the sight of God. The evil that David did was not a trivial one but adultery with a beautiful wife of Uriah was an abomination in the sight of the LORD.

David ordered that Uriah be placed the hot spot in the battlefield conspiring that he would be killed. As David planned Uriah was killed in the battlefield and David was responsible for this evil.

David repented of his sin but he was chastised. Nathan the prophet said to David that evil and

DAVID AND BATHSHEBA

sword shall not depart from his house. God has forgiven David's sin but David was never happy after committing adultery with Bathsheba and for the plot he laid for her husband's death. The LORD spoke to David through the prophet that sword shall depart from the house of his house and his wives shall be given to his neighbor who will lie with his wife openly to be known by everyone.

God said that David did sin in secret but He will punish him openly before all Israel and before the sun. King David was never had a happy life after this assertion by the prophet who spoke the word of the LORD (Ref: 2 Samuel 12:10-13).

In the very next chapter we read that evil entered into King David's house. King David's son Absalom had a beautiful sister named Tamar who wore colorful attire as was common for kings' daughters during those days.

Tamar was virgin and her beauty and her apparel attracted Amnon, who was half-brother of Absalom. David was their common father of Absalom and Amnon but their mothers were different.

Amnon fell in love with Tamar and lusted after her. Amnon's mind was never at ease after lusting after Tamar until he subdued her to satisfy his evil fleshly desire. Amnon' s evil thoughts made him sick to possess her at any cost.

Jonadab, a friend and a cousin of Amnon, inquired of him as to why was he lost his health and became lean and weak. Amnon explained to Jonadab that he loved Tamar and he wants her.

Jonadab (the son of Shimeah who was David's brother) was very cunning and subtil. The word 'subtil' was a translation of Hebrew Strong's number 6175. `aruwm which was used for the serpent who deceived the woman in the Garden of Eden.

"Now the serpent was more subtil than any beast of the field which the LORD God had made. And he said unto the woman, Yea, hath God said, Ye shall not eat of every tree of the garden?" (Genesis 3:1)

Jonadab had similar character of the serpent that deceived the woman in the Garden of Eden. The serpent spoke cunning words to the woman in the

Garden of Evil and the woman fell victim to the serpent. Jonadab infused evil thoughts into the mind of Amnon saying to him that he should lie down on bed and show that he was sick and when King David, his father, asks him as to why he was lying on the bed he should say that he was sick and that his sister Tamar should come to him to make couple of cakes and give to him that he may eat.

King David sent word for his daughter Tamar and asked her to go to her brother Amnon's house and feed him food. Tamar obeyed her father's instructions and went to her brother Amnon.

Tamar cooked food for Amnon her brother and gave it to him, but he refused to eat saying everyone in his house should go out and she may go with him into the chamber where he would eat food from her hand.

Everyone went out and Tamar took the cakes that she made for Amnon, her brother, who took hold of her and said to her "Come lie with me, my sister".

Amnon called her sister even when he was asking her to lie with him! Tamer said to Amnon, "Nay, my brother, do not force me; for no such thing ought to be done in Israel: do not thou this folly".

Tamar also admonished Amnon that he should not become a fool in Israel by committing such abomination.

Tamar pleaded Amnon to request King David to give her as Amnon's wife in marriage (which in those days was permissible; a case in point was that of Abraham and Sarah!), and that King would not refuse to give her as Amnon's wife. However, Amnon did not yield to the request made by Tamar but subdued her with his strength and raped her.

After this rape Amnon hated Tamar more intensely than how he loved her before. Amnon said to Tamar to get up and be gone! What an injustice Amnon had done.

First of all he should not have had her by his strength. Amnon' s intentions were wrong from the beginning. He loved Tamar only to satisfy his fleshly desire.

If he wanted her to be his wife, he should have asked King to give his daughter Tamar, who was his half-sister, which was legal during those days, but he preferred to rape her than to marry her.

According to Mosaic Law he deserved death by stoning. Surprisingly, David tried to suppress Mosaic law here and did not punish Amnon when he came to know of this evil that Amnon had done to Tamar.

Tamar said to Amnon, even before the King came to know of this evil, that Amnon was responsible for greater evil by letting her go instead of marrying her.

Tamar was innocent and helpful to her half-brother Amnon but he cheated her and sent her away. His rashness in sending her away after raping her was indeed a great deplorable act. He called his servant and said to him "Put now this woman out from me, and bolt the door after her".

Tamar had a colorful garment on her but when she was sent away from Amnon's house she put ashes on her head and rent her garment of various colors. She laid her hand on her head and cried. Tamar's brother Absalom came to know of the evil that his half-brother, Amnon did to her and consoled her to hold her peace. Tamar lived an isolated and fruitless devastated life in Absalom's house, thereafter.

Mosaic Law was very stringent. According to Mosaic Law the man committing such abomination as Amnon committed shall be put to death.

However, King David guilty of his own sin with Bathsheba, was wroth with Amnon but compromised on this issue and let his son Amnon go free from such punishment. David was King and he is supposed to protect his people, provide for his people and keep the Law of the land and God's law, but he compromised his principles here in letting his son Amnon go scot-free.

Absalom was supposed to take up severely with Amnon immediately after he came to know of the sin Amnon but he did let go his brother scot-free for two years. Absalom bore his vengeance in his heart and later killed Amnon.

CHAPTER 7
ABSALOM FLEES

Absalom fled to a heathen country after committing a cool blooded murder of his half-brother who raped his sister.

At a time when justice was to be sought in a permissible manner Absalom evaded such a course of action and harbored vengeance against his half-brother Amnon and got him killed by his servants in a feast arranged by him.

Unable to sustain the burden of the guilt and fear of his father David, King in Jerusalem, Absalom preferred to flee from Jerusalem to live in Geshur, an Armanian kingdom and he lived there for three years.

David was sore grieved over the death of Amnon his son, but after a while he was more concerned about Absalom, his son by another wife, than the death of Amnon.

Absalom was a very handsome man who stole the affection of his father. David's dilemma was highly pathetic. He was King in Jerusalem but his son Absalom was a fugitive running for his life. King has to render justice to his people but alas, he left first Amnon to go scot-free when he raped his daughter Tamar, and then now was in affection toward another son Absalom who deserved punitive action against him for scheming the death of Amnon.

Joab, a friend of David, intervened in these circumstances and sent a wise woman, who was a widow from 'Tekoah' to talk to king David. She, who had Joab's plans in her mind, was wise enough to project her guile rather than her pure wisdom to trap the king into her arguments and yield to her plea. When a person does not get justice in the lower courts he/she could approach the king's court for justice during those days.

The widow spoke to David and said to him that her husband was dead and she had two sons. One of her sons was killed by the other in the field while they fought with each other.

She said that her whole family rose against her to let her son be handed over to them to kill him as recompense to the offence he did to his brother.

David said to the woman to go home assuring her that he would take care of her case.

The woman praised the king and blessed his throne that it would be guiltless and her iniquity to be on her. David, the king assured her that her none of her son's hair would fall to the ground as the LORD lives.

The assurance by David to the woman in the name of the LORD was too much to think of. The woman took advantage of king's assurance to her and placed another question before the king as to how he did such a great favor to her while his son was banished to a distance place.

She quoted a wonderful thought to him that water spilt on the ground cannot be gathered up again; neither does God respect any person and in such a case there was no reason to keep his son, Absalom banished in a heathen country.

David understood that it was the plan of Joab to send her to him to seek the recall of Absalom to his own people and country.

The woman acknowledged her plea was made as a result of Job's intervention. The king accepted

Joab's request and accepted to get Absalom back to his home.

Joab fell to the ground and thanked the king. Joab went to Geshur and brought Absalom to Jerusalem. David the king said that Absalom may live in his home but not see the king's face. Absalom lived in Jerusalem but did not see king's face for two years.

Absalom was very handsome from the sole of his foot even up to his head and there was no blemish in him. His beauty was much praised in all the Israel and once every year he had his long hair cut because it was heavy on him. His hair equivalent to king's weight was sold for two hundred shekels (one shekel was equivalent to $8 to $12 – source Webster's dictionary). Absalom had three sons and a daughter. Surprisingly, he named his daughter after the name of his sister, Tamar, who was raped by his half-brother, Amnon, whom he killed in revenge.

Absalom's plans were quite subtle and revengeful. He kept silence when his sister Tamar was raped by Amnon but took revenge on him at a feast time in his own way. Now that he was in

Jerusalem and yet could not see the face of the king his plan was first to get attraction of Joab, and then have Israelites believe that he was a good man.

Bathsheba's first son by David was dead and the second son Solomon was alive but Absalom on one side and Adonijah, another son of David on the other had a quite crooked ideas to supplant David from kingship and occupy his position. Perhaps, Joab thought that Absalom, who was handsome, was the right one to replace king in due course of time.

It was Absalom's venture to try out a chance to see the king even though he was banished to see the countenance of king. Two years had elapsed after he came to Jerusalem and yet was not able to see the king who was his father. Absalom, therefore, forged ahead with a wicked plan of burning the barley plantation of Joab to get his attraction.

In spite of Absalom's two requests made to Joab to go and see him, yet Joab did not respond. Absalom, therefore, set on fire Joab's barley fields. Joab arose and went to Absalom and asked him as to why he set his fields on fire. Absalom responded saying that he sent word twice to Joab to go to him but he ignored his request, and, therefore, he set the fields of Joab on fire.

Absalom complained to Joab that it would have been better if he were there in Geshur. He said inasmuch Joab brought Absalom from Geshur he should make endeavors to help Absalom to see the king even if he were to kill him.

Joab, therefore, went to David and told him about Absalom's desire. David invited Absalom and Absalom went and made obeisance to the king David. David showed his love towards his son Absalom and kissed him.

In all these acts and more to come Absalom was trying to gain love, affection and favor from David and Israel. His ultimate motif was to gain power on Israel and become king.

After a while Absalom, after gaining courage, had fifty men to run before him while he rode chariots and horses. He stood at prominent place, a way of the gate to the city, and pretended as if he had the authority to stop anyone who came to seek justice in one's case before the king.

If any one came there the first person one would encounter was Absalom, who would ask one, which city one belonged to. When the one who came to justice answered Absalom saying that one was from Israel and revealed the city one belonged to, Absalom would say that the king was not there nor was any one there deputed to hear one's case.

Absalom would also say that if he were a judge in the land he would have every one's case would have come to him and he would have rendered justice. By enacting this drama each time Absalom stole the hearts of people in Israel.

It took forty years for Absalom to gain full control and win sympathy and love from Israel. After forty years were over Absalom called on the king and requested him that he may be allowed to go to Hebron to fulfill a vow. His vow, according to him, was that if God brought him back into Jerusalem from Geshur in Syria, he would serve the LORD.

The king was pleased with the request of Absalom and blessed him peace and conceded his request.

Absalom rose and went to Hebron but in the meanwhile by the perversion of his heart he sent spies throughout the all the tribes of Israel and said to them that when the trumpets were blown and as they hear the sound of the trumpets they shall say "Absalom is king in Hebron".

The conspiracy by Absalom against David, the king, who was his own father, increased with the courage he gained from the support of people of Israel who loved Absalom. David, who was so bold in all the actions he took earlier, loses his courage and flees from the conspiracy of Absalom.

CHAPETR 8
DAVID FLEES

"And David said unto all his servants that were with him at Jerusalem, Arise, and let us flee; for we shall not else escape from Absalom: make speed to depart, lest he overtake us suddenly, and bring evil upon us, and smite the city with the edge of the sword" (2 Samuel 15:14)

Absalom rebelled against David and pursued to kill him and take his seat as King. David sought help from God instead of pursuing Absalom. David was a man of wars and had won many wars with the help of God, but this time when his son pursued him he fled from him.

David was a shepherd boy before he became king and he was a good shepherd. When David was pleading his case with Saul he spoke of his courageous acts in killing a lion and a bear. He had faith that the Lord who delivered him from the paw of the lion would deliver him from Philistine giant, Goliath as well. Indeed David was triumphant in the battle (1 Samuel 17:33-37). But here, we see David fleeing from Absalom.

In Psalms Chapter 3 we see David recollecting increase in number of those that troubled him. His enemies ridiculed him saying that there was no hope for him in God. Selah – (pause and think!).

David cried unto the Lord and the Lord heard him out of his holy hill. David slept peacefully and woke up and praised him with confidence that he will not be afraid of ten thousands of people. (Psalms 3:4-5). Indeed good sleep is a blessing from God and rising up from good sleep is equally a blessing from God.

David went on praying to God to save his life. He recollected before God that God helped him to smite his enemies upon their cheek bone and he had broken the teeth of the ungodly. He also proclaimed that salvation belongs to the Lord.

Absalom was handsome and wise enough to gather the support of people. At the time when Absalom was pursuing David he was loved by people and David was ridiculed and hated. Lord Jesus Christ was also ridiculed and hated by people and they crucified him. They said to Jesus to come down from the cross and save himself and save them as well.

"He saved others; himself he cannot save. If he be the King of Israel, let him now come down from the cross, and we will believe him" (Matthew 27:42)

Jesus could have prayed to the Father to help to get off the cross and he would have had twelve legions of angels to fight for him; but then the purpose of Jesus coming to this earth was not to fight but to pay the price for our sin. (Matthew 26:53)

Similar was the case when David was in trouble. Conspiracy increased and David got the information that the hearts of men of Israel were after Absalom (2 Samuel 15:13). Yet, David commanded Joab, Abishai and Ittai that they should deal with Absalom gently. (2 Samuel 18:5)

Apostle Paul wrote in Romans 12:19 "Dearly beloved, avenge not yourselves, but rather give place unto wrath: for it is written, Vengeance is mine; I will repay, saith the Lord".

The end for Absalom was not good. Absalom was riding a mule and his head caught hold of the oak and he was hanging between the heaven and earth.

The mule went away. Later, Joab came and thrust three darts into Absalom's heart but he was still alive and Absalom faced death at the hands of ten young men who smote him and slew him. (2 Samuel 18:15)

David inquired Cushi whether Absalom was safe or not and when he did not receive a favorable reply David cried that it would have been better if his life was paid as ransom to save his son.

"And the king was much moved, and went up to the chamber over the gate, and wept: and as he went, thus he said, O my son Absalom, my son, my son Absalom! would God I had died for thee, O Absalom, my son, my son!" (2 Samuel 18:33)

In comparison, our Lord Jesus Christ loved us and paid price for our salvation that whoever believes in him shall not perish but will have everlasting life.

CHAPTER 9
ADONIJAH AND SOLOMON

Adonijah, had a greater right to the throne than Solomon, yet he was not the one chosen by God. He also attempted to usurp the throne in an unruly and wrong way, which resulted in his dethronement.

Solomon not only spared his life, but gave him possessions. He thus established his throne by mercy. Let us examine ourselves if we are in such situation today. If we are not chosen by God, we might have to seek the refuge later and seek mercy of those who are chosen by God.

Let us remember that the coveted positions are for those, who are chosen by God; not for those who try to usurp. God will cause the usurpers to end in seeking refuge and will send them to retired life. Only those chosen by God will attain the coveted positions and do the will of God

Here is a story in 1kings 1st chapter. David's first four sons were, Amnon, Chileab, Absalom, and Adonijah. He also had a son through Bathsheba, and that was Solomon. 2nd Samuel chapter 13:28, 29 and chapter 18:24 show the violent deaths Amnon and Absalom suffered. Chileab, must have died in childhood.

Adonijah, the son of David, usurped the throne of David. He began his plotting with the gain of allies; (1) Joab, who David was unable to control, (2) Abiathar the Priest. Adonijah's next scheme was to host feast for his supporters. Vs. 5 reads "...I will be king; and prepared him chariots and horsemen to run before him."

David did not know the plotting and the scheming Adonijah was going ahead with. With the help of Abiathar the priest he usurped the kingship. He slew sheep and oxen and fat cattle, called all his brethren the king's sons and all the men of Judah, the king's servants and hosted feast. And he started reigning.

Bathsheba went in unto the king David, did obeisance and told him, about that his throne was usurped by Adonijah. Bathsheba reminded him of his swearing that his son, Solomon, through her, would become the king. While she was yet talking to her husband, David the king, Nathan the prophet came in.

Nathan questioned the king if he had at any time said that Adonijah would become king. He explained to the king how Adonijah, usurped the kingship without sending an invitation to Nathan, the prophet or Zadok, the priest and Benaiah the son of Jehoida, and Solomon.

David rises up then, and says, "Assuredly Solomon thy son shall reign after me, and he shall sit upon my throne in my stead; even so will I certainly do this day". Bathsheba thanked the king.

King David called Zadok the priest, and Nathan the prophet, and Benaiah the son of Jehoida, and in their presence caused Solomon, his son, to sit upon his mule and ride to "Gihon".

Later Zadok, the priest and Nathan the priest anointed Solomon. And, Benaiah the son of Jehoida answered the king, and said, Amen; the LORD God of my lord the king says so too. As the LORD hath been with my Lord the king, even so be with Solomon, and make his throne greater than the throne of my lord king David. Thus became Solomon the official king over Israel.

Ref: 2 Samuel Chapters 14 and 15 1 Kings Chapter 1

CHAPPTER 10
DAVID THANKS GOD

Wherefore David blessed the LORD before all the congregation: and David said, Blessed be thou, LORD God of Israel our father, for ever and ever". (1 Chronicles 29:10)

King David was blessed by God and he in turn thanks and praises God. This is the first time the God of Israel is addressed as "father".

David blesses God of Israel and wishes that His kingdom, His greatness, His power, His glory, His victory and majesty be for ever and ever. David praises God that the Name of the Lord be exalted as head above all. (1 Chronicles 29:10-15)

In his own life, David saw that both riches and honor come from God, who rules over all. David acknowledges that in the hand of the living God is power and might, and it is He who makes one great, and gives strength to all. He saw in his own life, he defeated Philistine giant Goliath.

Before that he killed a lion and a bear to protect his sheep. Our Lord Jesus Christ is the good shepherd and we are his sheep. We all had gone astray but Jesus had mercy on us.

"For ye were as sheep going astray; but are now returned unto the Shepherd and Bishop of your souls". (1 Peter 2:25)

David was a good shepherd and saved his sheep from peril and death. In all the wars that he fought it was the hand of God that he saw and he was not hesitant to acknowledge that God was his rock of refuge, and because God helped him he had victories.

David humbled himself and said that all things came from God. He set apart huge wealth for the construction of the Temple at Jerusalem. David ardently desired to build a Temple for God, but God did not permit him to build it, but said to David that his son, Solomon, would build the Temple at Jerusalem because David was a man of wars.

David acknowledged that he and his people were strangers in the land and they were sojourners, just as his fathers were. He says his days on the earth were as shadow which does not last.

Lord Jesus Christ, who is called "the Last Adam", fought with our enemy, the Old Dragon that deceived Adam and Eve.

"And so it is written, The first man Adam was made a living soul; the last Adam was made a quickening spirit". (1 Corinthians 15:45)

Jesus showed us the way to have everlasting life. He defeated Satan at the Cross and whoever accepts this fact and accepts Jesus as his Lord will have everlasting life.

We too are strangers and sojourners on this earth. Our eternal inheritance is in heaven. As the born-again children of our God, we have been blessed with heavenly blessings and we will be in New Jerusalem that comes down from heaven.

"And I John saw the holy city, new Jerusalem, coming down from God out of heaven, prepared as a bride adorned for her husband". (Revelation 21:2)

Lord Jesus Christ taught his disciples to pray and asked them to start the prayer beginning with the words, "Our Father, who art in heaven, hallowed be thy name".

David said: "The fear of the LORD is the beginning of wisdom: a good understanding have all they that do his commandments: his praise endureth forever". (Psalms 111:10)

The beginning to becoming great in any one' life starts with honoring, praising, and blessing the name of God. Unless and until God blesses us we cannot have anything. Except the Lord build the house the laborers build it in vain.

"Except the LORD build the house, they labour in vain that build it: except the LORD keep the city, the watchman waketh but in vain". (Psalms 127:1)

Apostle Paul says:

"But my God shall supply all your need according to his riches in glory by Christ Jesus" (Philippians 4:19)

CHAPTER 11
DAVID HONORED GOD

David depended upon God before waging wars. Before he went for war against Philistines he enquired of the Lord saying "Shall I go up to the Philistines?" and God asked him to go ahead.

"And David enquired of the LORD, saying, Shall I go up to the Philistines? wilt thou deliver them into mine hand? And the LORD said unto David, Go up: for I will doubtless deliver the Philistines into thine hand" (2 Samuel 5:19)

David not only put an end to Philistines who troubled the children of Israel but he also defeated Moabites. He also defeated Hadadezer, the son of Rehob, king of Zobab and recovered his border at the river Euphrates.

David smote Syrians and they became servants to David and brought gifts. Edomites also became servants of David and the Almighty God preserved David wherever he went. (2 Samuel 8:14)

David dedicated unto God the silver and gold that he had from all nations which he subdued. David's administration and organization was excellent. David administered judgment and justice to all people. (2 Samuel 8:11,15 and 18)

"And David reigned over all Israel; and David executed judgment and justice unto all his people" (2 Samuel 8:15)

King David's sincere worship of God is seen in many references. He thought of building a temple for God but God allowed his son Solomon to build the temple at Jerusalem.

Speaking to Solomon David said that it was in his mind to build a house unto the name of God, but God said to him that David had shed blood abundantly upon the earth in His sight, and made great wars, and, therefore, he should not build a house unto His name.

God said that his son Solomon would build a house unto the name of the Lord. God promised that He would establish Solomon's throne forever over Israel.

He wished that God may give wisdom and understanding to Solomon to keep the law of the Lord. David assured Solomon that if he kept the law of the Lord, he would prosper.

He encouraged his son to be of good courage, not to dread, or dismayed. David helped him and said:

"Now, behold, in my trouble I have prepared for the house of the LORD an hundred thousand talents of gold, and a thousand talents of silver; and of brass and iron without weight; for it is in abundance: timber also and stone have I prepared; and thou mayest add thereto" (1 Chronicles 22:14)

God honors who honor him. God blessed David and Solomon abundantly.

Bible says every man is come short of the glory of God and there is none that has not sinned. If anyone says he is not a sinner he is a liar. (cf. Romans 3:23, 1 John 1:10).

If that is the case then there is reason to condemn David for his lapses. David repented of his sin.

David honored God. David obeyed the word God. Saul did not honor God and he was rebellious.

No wonder he was removed by God from his kingship and his kingdom was given to David, who became king in his stead. That is the reason why God called David as a man after mine own heart who fulfills His will in its entirety.

"And when he had removed him, he raised up unto them David to be their king; to whom also he gave testimony, and said, I have found David the son of Jesse, a man after mine own heart, which shall fulfill all my will". (Acts 13:22)

CHAPTER 12
MEPHIBOSHETH

Two Kings in contrast in Old Testament were those who very often we speak of. One was King Saul and another King David. King Saul was rejected by God, while King David was accepted by God.

King Saul sought after the life of David. Saul's daughter was David's wife, yet Saul was after the life of David. Jonathan was the son of Saul. Jonathan was not only a close relative of David, but was his good friend. Jonathan's son was Mephibosheth.

Mephibosheth was very unfortunate in his life, because when he was just a child of five years, his nurse dropped him off her hands, and he became crippled and lame in his both legs.

Jonathan knew that David was chosen one of God and, therefore, requested David, to have mercy on his family. David was extremely kind to Saul's family even though Saul sought after his soul very often.

David asked Mephibosheth if there was anyone left in the family of Saul, that he could show mercy.

Mephibosheth compared himself to a dead dog and inquired David, why he wanted to show kindness. The word, "Dog" is a repulsive and most detested one used in the Bible. Mephibosheth compared himself as not only a dog but dead one.

We see David's kindness was so great that he not only gave Mephibosheth, his inheritance, but also granted him the privilege to dine with him, on his table, along with him, throughout his life.

But God, who is rich in mercy, for his great love wherewith he loved us, Even when we were dead in sins, hath quickened us together with Christ, (by grace ye are saved;) (Ephesians 2:4-5)

And if children, then heirs; heirs of God, and joint-heirs with Christ; if so be that we suffer with him, that we may be also glorified together. (Romans 8:17)

In Jesus Christ we see a greater love than this. He offered his own life for our sake and granted us salvation free of cost. He says, "Behold I stand at the door and knock. If anyone hears My voice and opens the door, I will come in to him and dine with him, and he with Me." (Revelation 3:20).

Lord Jesus Christ also said, "I am the living bread which came down from heaven. If anyone eats this bread, he will live forever; and the bread that I shall give is My flesh, which I gave for the life of the world." (John 6:51)

Mephibosheth received inheritance and a place at the king David's table. Jesus calls us to receive our inheritance and have eternal life.

Is there still anyone, who reads this message in need of the favor of Jesus Christ? Salvation is free of cost. Jesus paid the price for our sins. We only need to ask him forgiveness and accept Him as personal savior. (cf. II Samuel 9th chapter)

CHAPTER 13
SECURITY OF BELIEVER IN CHRIST

But God commendeth his love toward us, in that, while we were yet sinners, Christ died for us". (Romans Ch. 5:8)

While we were enemies to God Christ died for our sake. He loved us and had compassion on us. God is not human to take back the gift that He gives to believer in him.

It is by hearing the Word of God that the sinner confesses his sins and trusts in the Lord. He lays his faith in God through Jesus Christ. It is the Father in heaven, who draws unto himself, those that are to be saved.

Such faith comes by hearing the Word of God. He who receives Jesus as his personal savior is secure in God's arms. Holy Spirit leads the believer every day and guides his paths.

Eph. Ch 2:8-10 show us that this gift of salvation cannot be gained through any amount of works of man. No man can boast that he received salvation by doing good works but good works follow after a man has received salvation. We are the workmanship of God. Any sin is abominable to God and no sin will go unpaid for while the believer is on this earth.

Salvation is the gift of God:

The gift of God is so precious that once it is given to a believer God cannot deny His own love toward us, nor can He deny His love toward His One and only Son, Jesus Christ that He takes back that gift from us.

Romans 6:23 is a very familiar verse in the Bible. There is one great gift that God gave unto us through His One and Only Son Jesus Christ and that gift is the salvation and it is the greatest gift of all.

Wages are the earnings for the work done by someone. Bible calls the wages of sin is death, but the gift of God is eternal life through Jesus Christ our Lord.

The Father in heaven in His mercy sent His One and Only Son Jesus Christ because He loved us first, even when we were dead in our trespasses and saved us by grace.

Salvation can neither be earned through the works nor can it be purchased for a price. It is the gift of God through Lord Jesus Christ. He paid the price for our sins upon the cross of Calvary. He shed His precious blood for our sake and washed our sins in His blood.

The love of God is so great that He found us in our trespasses and sent His One and Only Son, Jesus Christ for our sake, that whosoever believes in Him shall not perish but will have everlasting life.

If we confess our sins, He is faithful and just to forgive us our sins. He sought us because He loved us first. We received salvation not because we loved Him first, but because He loved us first.

THE CHARGE:

There are those who charge that salvation of a believer can be lost if he commits sin in his day-to-day life; but this charge is untenable. Salvation of a believer is secure and eternal.

The work of God rendered through His One and only begotten Son, Lord Jesus Christ in extending His grace toward us is everlasting one. He will not take back the salvation from any recipient on any reason.

We are sealed with the Holy Spirit unto redemption. An important fact that should be borne in mind is that a true believer will not sin but will stand firm in his faith in the Lord.

The Scriptures say that one that commits sin is of the devil and one that is born of God does not commit sin (1 John 3:8-9).

Anyone who confesses his sins to God and believes that the Son of God, Lord Jesus Christ, died for him and rose from the dead will have salvation and he will have everlasting life.

No temptation is beyond our capacity of tolerance:

"There hath no temptation taken you but such as is common to man: but God is faithful, who will not suffer you to be tempted above that ye are able; but will with the temptation also make a way to escape, that ye may be able to bear it" (1 Corinthians 10:13)

No temptation has ever over taken any believer that he could not find an alternative way to escape from such temptation.

God provides alternative way so that the believer may not fall into sin and perish. In spite of such provision available, if believer commits sins he will receive chastisement from God and suffers in this world. Because he would not be working for the Lord he would lose his rewards also.

Salvation is never lost because believer is sealed with the Holy Spirit. It is the gift of God and it is a firm promise from God that he will uphold us and no one can pluck us from out his hand. God will not break His promises.

THE LOVE OF GOD

Apostle Paul says in Romans 8:33-39 that no one can separate us from the love of God. Lord Jesus ascended into heaven after forty days of his resurrection from the dead and he is seated on the right hand of the Majesty.

He is pleading with the Father on behalf of us who have salvation Him. The fact that our Lord Jesus is interceding on behalf of us with the Father in heaven without ceasing is another reason to believe that believer is secure and his salvation is secure.

Otherwise, it would mean that the intercession of the only begotten Son, Jesus Christ, on behalf of us is in vain and has no effect.

The Holy Spirit guides and convicts the believer of his failings every moment. The feign thoughts that God, the Father in heaven, can deny the intercession Jesus Christ are too presumptuous to be taken as true. The salvation given to a believer as a merciful gift by His grace will not be taken back.

Every believer should keep in mind that there are rewards for him for the works he does for God after receiving salvation. The rewards are given at the "Judgment seat of Christ" (which is also known as "Bema Seat of Christ") in the mid-air.

The believer, who has truly tasted that love from God, cannot think of falling into sin again and

again to repent repeatedly. It would mean
crucifying Lord Jesus afresh repeatedly and
putting Him to open shame.

Hebrews 6:4-6 reminds us of this fact that a
believer, who received the gift of salvation will not
think of falling into sin every day to seek refuge
under the provisions in the Scriptures about
security of the salvation. He would rather lead a
holy life pleasing unto the Lord.

GOD HAS CHOSEN US

Speaking to His disciples, Jesus said that He
would no longer call them as 'servants', but would
call them as friends. The disciples did not become
the disciples of Jesus by their own choice, but it
was Jesus, who chose them as His disciples. He
ordained that they should go and bring forth fruit
unto the Lord.

The words of Lord Jesus Christ help us to
understand that the salvation of a believer in
Christ is secure and eternal. Jesus' own words as
recorded in John 10:29 are beyond doubt that He
holds us firm in his fold.

"My Father, which gave them me, is greater than all; and no man is able to pluck them out of my Father's hand". (John 10:29)

"Herein is love, not that we loved God, but that he loved us, and sent his Son to be the propitiation for our sins. (1 John 4:10)

Jesus also promised His disciples that whatever they ask of the Father in heaven in His name, He would give unto them. They did not belong to this world, and because they did not belong to the world, Jesus chose them. (John 15:16) Whoever receives Jesus as his/her personal Savior, to them God gave power to become the sons of God (John 1:12).

Jesus gives eternal life to all those, who believe in Him, so that they shall never perish, nor can anyone pluck the believer out of His hand. The Word of God is so clear here in John 10:28-30 that no one can pluck a believer out of His hand.

"And I give unto them eternal life; and they shall never perish, neither shall any man pluck them out of my hand. My Father, which gave them me, is greater than all; and no man is able to pluck them out of my Father's hand. I and my Father are one". (John 10:28-30)

A believer can trust in the words of Lord Jesus Christ, just as Apostle Paul affirmed in Romans 8:38-39, that neither anyone or any act, or any power, can separate us from the love of God, because we are in Christ Jesus and let us, therefore, give thanks unto the Father in heaven, just as Apostle Paul asked us to do in Colossians 1:1-13.

God made us partakers in the inheritance of the saints in light and delivered from the power of darkness in order to translate us into the Kingdom of His One and Only Son, Jesus Christ.

We believe in the gospel of Jesus Christ and about the eternal life that Jesus promised to us and we are sealed with the Holy Spirit of promise.

We are purchased possession of our God so that we may be unto him the praise of his glory. We should bear in mind the hope of our calling, and know "what the riches of the glory of his inheritance in the saints" (Eph.1:13-18)

THE SEVERITY OF JUDGMENT

The writer of Hebrews warns about the severity of the judgment of God that falls on those that sin willfully trampling down the sacrifice of our Only High Priest, Lord Jesus Christ and apostatizes.

Hebrews 10:26-31 deal with this dilemma that Christians attribute to salvation being lost in case a believer in Christ commits sin.

These verses show us the importance of realizing who the Son of God is, and the results deliberate denial and renunciation of the faith in Christ fetches.

In the Old Testament the greatest of all punishments was awarded to deliberate denial of the Word of the LORD. "Because he hath despised the word of the LORD, and hath broken his commandment, that soul shall utterly be cut off; his iniquity shall be upon him" (Numbers 15:31).

Such punishment is awarded to those, who deliberately renounce the Son of God and tread Him down under foot.

The recognition of the efficacy of the blood of Jesus Christ and his High Priest-hood stands out to be the dominant demand from anyone in the world. One that is saved will never renounce Lord Jesus Christ and the efficacy of His blood shed upon the cross of Calvary.

It is, therefore, beyond doubt that only unbeliever can tread down the Son of God under his feet and face the serious consequences of being thrown into the 'lake of fire'.

The believer in Christ is secure eternally inasmuch as his belief in Lord Jesus Christ as his personal savior involves inseparable union with Christ and the death to sin (Romans 6:6-8).

If any believer in Christ strives to trample upon the Son of God and denies Him, God will make him kneel down on his feet with enough chastisement, and acknowledge that Jesus is the Lord, and reaffirm that He is the Savior.

CHAPTER 14
REDEEMED FROM BONDAGE OF SIN

So also is the resurrection of the dead. It is sown in corruption; it is raised in incorruption: (1 Corinthians 15:42)

Bible says we were dead in trespasses and sins; but to those who believed in Jesus Christ as personal savior, it is the quickening of the spirit. We, who are born again, are redeemed from the bondage of sin. We are saved unto eternal life.

Sin held us as slaves; made us blind to the truth of the Gospel of Jesus Christ; made us liable for condemnation; had us as aliens from the commonwealth of Israel; strangers to the covenants of promise; had us in a state of hopelessness, and it treated us a strangers and foreigners to the living God.

God delivered us and made us servants of righteousness. We, who were the children of wrath are given the privilege of calling the living

God, as 'Abba, Father'. He has given us the privilege of be called as sons of God. He has translated us into the Kingdom of His dear Son.

Dead in trespasses does not mean that a man is fully dead in all respects to the extent that he cannot believe on Jesus, but it means that Satan has blinded his belief and understanding to the extent that the Scriptural truth appears to him as foolishness. (Ref: Eph 2nd Chapter, 2 Cor. 4:3-4, Romans 6:17-18, John 3:19-20, Mark 2:17, Luke 15th Chapter, Col 1:13)

The only requirement that God has placed on a sinner is to repent of his sins and call on Jesus to forgive his/her sins. Entire price for redemption from sinful life is paid for by Jesus on the cross.

There is nothing that a sinner needs to do except believing in the blood of Jesus, who paid the price for our redemption already.

God formed our bodies with the dust of the ground. When he created the first man, on this earth he breathed his life into the nostrils of the man and the man (Adam) became a living soul.

The living soul that God created was in the image of God.

After man had committed sin he lost that image of God, and 'death reigned from Adam to Moses even over that had not sinned after the similitude of Adam's transgression'.

By the offence of one many came under the penalty of death, but by the gift of God that is 'grace' many have become eligible to receive eternal life. It was by one, (Adam), who sinned that death came to reign on man, and it is by the ONE (Jesus), that the gift of God is available for all sinners.

All those who accept that the Son of God, Jesus, died for his/her sins, and accept him as the 'Lord' of one's life are saved from damnation. It is then that the soul dead in trespasses is redeemed; it is then that the soul is delivered from suffering the wrath of God. The soul that does not repent of his/her sins will be cast into lake of fire, by God, after the 'Great white throne judgment', which is the final judgment.

As and when our earthly house of this tabernacle gets dissolved we gain a building of God, the house not made with hands, but that which would be eternal in heaven.

We groan in this body desiring to be clothed upon with the house that we would have in heavens, and that glorified body, which resurrects from the dead, when Jesus comes again, would not be naked; but the living soul with eternal life that does not marry nor is given in marriage. (Ref: 2 Corinthians. 5th Chapter of Matthew22:30 and Romans 5th Chapter.)

Apostle Peter reveals a marvelous truth in 1 Peter 1st Chapter. Addressing to the strangers scattered throughout Pontus, Galatia, Cappadocia, Asia and Bithynia he calls on Elect by God the Father, and wishes them 'Grace'.

All those, whom he addressed were, as he says, were begotten unto lively hope by the resurrection of Jesus Christ from the dead and to inherit incorruptible, and undefiled rewards that do not fade away. These are reserved for them in heaven.

If we read 2 Timothy 3:16 it says, 'All scripture is given by inspiration of God, and is profitable for doctrine, for reproof, for correction, for instruction in righteousness'.

Depending upon 2 Timothy 3:16 every one, irrespective of his belonging to the clan of Jews or Gentiles can claim this verse to be applicable in one's life, provided he/she has accepted Jesus Christ as his/her personal Savior.

The power of God keeps us and assures us that inheritance, which is in heaven. We have the eternal life to be with the Lord Jesus Christ always. That inheritance is incorruptible, and undefiled. It does not fade away.

We may face trials and tribulations in this world, but the rewards that are reserved for us in eternity are great and beyond description.

If we call on the Father, He will help us to pass our pilgrimage on this earth in fear of Him, rendering to Him His due worship. We are not redeemed by silver or gold, but by the blood of His only begotten Son Jesus Christ, whom John identified as the Lamb of God. Peter confirms that this Lamb of God was Lord Jesus. John said this is the Lamb of God came to this world to take away the sin of the world.

The Father in heaven judges every man according to his/her works while sojourning on this earth. He keeps record of our vain conversations that we may have received from our earthly fathers following traditions.

Therefore, let us keep in mind that as the Scripture says, Lord Jesus Christ was 'foreordained before the foundation of the world' and he was revealed unto us in the form of man. He died on the cross, bearing our sins, so that we may have redemption from sin.

God raised him from the dead on the third day after crucifixion. Jesus is not dead lying in the grave just as any other man; but he was raised from the dead on the third day as prophesied.

Later, after forty days on this earth he ascended into heaven. He is now seated on the right hand of the Majesty, pleading on our behalf with the Father.

Our faith in God increases as our days pass on this earth because of this infallible truth.

Our souls are purified by believing on this truth and hope increases as our sojourning on this earth tapers to start afresh eternal life with the only one, who paid the price for our salvation.

Likewise, our love for one another should be fervent and pure. Just as grass withers, and flower fades, our life on this earth is also temporal and temporary, but the life with Jesus is eternal as the Word of God endures forever. (I Peter 1st Chapter)

Apostle Paul warned (in Romans 1st Chapter) all those Romans that they had changed the glory of the un-corruptible God into images of God's creation. They made beasts and creeping things and made them as their own gods.

Therefore, 'God also gave them up to uncleanness through the lusts of their own hearts to dishonor their own bodies between themselves'.

But for those, who honor Lord Jesus Christ and take refuge in him, there is hope that they will rise from the dead unto incorruption. The body of the believer in Christ is raised in power, even though on this earth he/she was in weakness. The believer in Christ rises in an incorruptible body that has natural body and also spiritual body. The first man Adam was made a living soul and the last Adam (Jesus) was made a quickening spirit. 1 Corinthians 15:42-45

It is a great blessing because we, who were dead in trespasses and sins, are also quickened.

"And you hath he quickened, who were dead in trespasses and sins" Ephesians 2:1"

CHAPTER 15
THOUSAND YEAR REIGN

John saw in his vision an angel coming down from heaven holding the key of the abyss and a huge chain in his hand. The angel conquered Satan that cheated Eve and bound him and cast him into that abyss for thousand years in order that he may not deceive any one.

John was given an understanding that Satan will be let loose for a short period of time after the thousand-year-rule by Jesus Christ is completed. The angel put a seal on the bottom-less pit where Satan was bound and the angel shuts him up in the abyss.

Then John saw that there were thrones. He saw that judgment was given unto those who sat upon them. He saw the souls of martyrs of those who stood for Jesus and for the word of God.

He also saw those who did not worship Antichrist, or his image, or received the mark of the beast either on their hands or on their foreheads. They all lived and reigned with Christ for thousand years.

These are those who faced Great Tribulation under Antichrist and successfully come out from his atrocious rule.

Antichrist promises peace for seven years but after three and half years he breaks covenant and there will be great tribulation. Jews will be cheated by his false promises.

After facing Great Tribulation the Jews will call upon Jesus to save them and they will accept Jesus as their Messiah.

They live and reign with Christ for thousand years. This is the period when Jesus rules literally from the throne of David from Jerusalem and there would be peace everywhere. Satan will not be active at that period of time.

During the period of Antichrist the Jews face tremendous torture that surpasses any kind of tribulation, harassment, or torture faced by anybody in the world from the beginning.

The Jews need help during this time. They are the "brethren" of our Lord Jesus Christ who was himself a Jew. There are three classes mentioned in Matthew Chapter 25. They are the "Sheep", the "Goats" and the "brethren".

To the category of the Sheep belong those who help during the Great Tribulation period the "brethren" of Jesus Christ and to the category of the Goats belong those who have neglected Jews during the Great Tribulation period.

When Jesus descends from the mid-air after the completion of seven-year period of Antichrist's rule, he steps on the Mount of Olives which is before Jerusalem.

The Mount of Olives cleaves in the midst towards the east and the west, resulting in a very great valley. Half of the mountain shall be removed toward the north and half toward the south. (Zechariah 14:4). This Valley is called "Valley of Jehoshaphat". (Joel 3:1-2)

There was no such place as "Valley of Jehoshaphat" before or now is in Israel, but there will be such place in the future. The word "Jehoshaphat" means "The Lord Judges".

This is the throne of Jesus from where he judges the nations on this earth. Here he will gather all the nations to judge. Those whom Jesus justifies as having helped his "brethren" and those Jews who have accept Jesus as Messiah during Great Tribulation period will enter into literal thousand year reign by Lord Jesus Christ.

Jesus says to the nations who have helped his "brethren" "Verily I say unto you, Inasmuch as ye have done it unto one of the least of these my brethren, ye have done it unto me."

Those whom Jesus does not justify as having helped the "brethren" during Great Tribulation will not be in the thousand year rule by Jesus Christ, but will be cast out. Jesus says to them "Depart from me, ye cursed, into everlasting fire, prepared for the devil and his angels".

We who are in the Church saved by the grace of God, having been washed in the blood of Jesus Christ will be with Him for ever and ever in bodies that are transformed in a twinkling of an eye at the last trump (Ref. 1 Corinthians 15:52).

This happens when the trumpet sounds when the Lord himself shall descend from heaven as recorded in 1 Thessalonians 4:16-17

CHAPTER 16
DAVID'S THRONE ESTABLISHED
FOR EVER

Houses made of wooden were considered as posh living Houses in the Old Testament period, more so, if they were made of Cedar wood. King David was living in such a house made of Cedar wood (2 Samuel 5:11).

One day David expressed his concern to Nathan the prophet that while he himself was living in a house made of Cedar wood the Ark of God was within the curtains (2 Samuel 7:2).

King David had an intention to build a house for God. The prophet, although he was from God, spoke this time instantaneously without seeking counsel from God and said that the King may do what was in his mind. But God spoke to Nathan the prophet and asked him to go and question David, if he is capable of building a house for God to dwell in!

God spoke to David through Nathan the prophet that all along when the children of Israel journeyed from Egypt to Canaan God did not have any place to dwell in except for a tent and a tabernacle.

God questioned if He asked at any time from any of the tribes of Israel any favor to build a Cedar house for Himself. God reminded David that He gave all the instructions and commandments from a tent and from tabernacle.

God asked David to recollect his own position from where he was made to rise. David was a mere shepherd and yet God made him ruler over the children of Israel and not only God was with him but God made his name to be greater than any king upon this earth.

All his enemies were cut out of his sight and his name was made great like that of great men who were on the earth.

God said that he will appoint a place for his people Israel and plant them that they would dwell in a place of their own.

God assured that He would not allow wicked people to afflict the children of Israel any more as they did before. After bringing the children of

Israel from out of Egypt into Canaan God commanded judges to be over his people Israel and later David was made the King.

God caused David to rest from all his enemies. God told David that He will make a house for David and when his days are fulfilled he will sleep with his fathers. God promised to set up David's seed and establish his kingdom forever.

God indicated that King Solomon will build a house for God's name and establish his throne of his kingdom forever.

God said that if Solomon committed any iniquity he would chastise him with rod of men, and with the stripes of the children of men, but His mercy will not depart from him.

King David humbled himself after hearing God's word through Nathan the prophet and exalted the name of God by saying:

"Wherefore thou art great, O LORD God: for there is none like thee, neither is there any God beside thee, according to all that we have heard with our ears" (2 Samuel 7:22)

"And let thy name be magnified forever, saying, The LORD of hosts is the God over Israel: and let the house of thy servant David be established before thee" (2 Samuel 7:26)

CHAPTER 17
JERUSALEM WILL BE CALLED BY A NEW NAME

The Holy city Jerusalem, the city of our Lord, is now, not in good shape. The city will be called "Hephzibah", and its land "Beulah".

The Lord delights in making the city delightful for everyone and the land like married woman. (Isaiah Ch. 62:4). This is a prophecy about the status of Jerusalem in the millennial kingdom of Jesus.

Lord Jesus Christ is the Messiah. The Jews rejected him and called upon themselves the blood of Jesus in order that he may be crucified (Matthew 27:24-25). Peter's speech testifies about those who crucified Jesus.

"Ye men of Israel, hear these words; Jesus of Nazareth, a man approved of God among you by miracles and wonders and signs, which God did by him in the midst of you, as ye yourselves also know: Him, being delivered by the determinate counsel and foreknowledge of God, ye have taken, and by wicked hands have crucified and slain" (Acts 2:22-23)

Indeed, they paid the price in AD 70 according to historians. Earlier, they worshipped idols many-a-time and were chastised by God. They rebelled against God and paid the price for their actions. Yet, they are his people; the city of David is his city.

Like Boaz, who was kinsman redeemer of Ruth, Jesus is our redeemer. He came into this world, died for our sins, was buried, rose from the dead on the third day and later ascended into heaven. He is seated on the right hand of the Majesty and interceding for us.

We, who are redeemed by the blood of Christ, are greater than the unrepentant Jews. But for those, who have accepted Jesus as their personal savior, there is no condemnation irrespective of their race, ethnicity, color, or creed.

Lord Jesus, who is the messiah, speaks and says that he will not sit quite, nor will he rest until he redeems city of Jerusalem again. He defeats the kings loyal to Antichrist at "Armageddon", and sits on the throne of David and literally rules.

In the thousand years of his rule there shall be perfect peace. Satan will be bound with chains and thrown into abyss by an angel who comes from heaven. Later Satan will be released for a short time when he goes Gog and Magog to deceive the nations but fire from God comes down from heaven and devours Satan. (Revelation Ch. 20:8)

The dead who did not accept Jesus Christ as their personal savior will resurrect at that time. The Lord shall judge them at the 'Great white throne' and cast them along with death, hell, and the devil and his angels into the 'lake of fire' to be tormented for ever and ever. This is the second death.

For those who are saved, there is no second death but they will have everlasting life to be with the Lord for ever and ever.

Note here when Antichrist and false prophet are thrown into the lake of fire! It is before the devil that deceived!!! Revelation 20:10 confirms it.

When the devil was cast into the lake of fire, the Antichrist and the false prophet were already there in the lake of fire.

These are only the ones who will be in the lake of fire before the 'Great White Throne Judgment' (Revelation 16:16 and Revelation 20:8-10).

Does the Scripture say anybody is thrown into the lake of fire before Antichrist and false prophet? No, not at all!

There shall come out of heaven a New Jerusalem and we, who are saved, shall be in that Holy City. The Church is the bride of our Lord Jesus Christ.

Lord Jesus says that he has set watchmen upon the walls of Jerusalem and they will not keep quite nor will sleep but keep a watch over the city and will make the city a praise of the earth.

This is a promise of Messiah and he has sworn by his right hand and by the arm of his strength. Messiah promised that no more the enemies of Jerusalem will eat its corn as their food no stranger will ever drink its wine. Gentiles will see its righteousness and kings will glory.

"And the Gentiles shall see thy righteousness, and all kings thy glory: and thou shalt be called by a new name, which the mouth of the LORD shall name." (Isaiah 62:2)

CHAPTER 18
MESSAGE OF CROSS

"For the preaching of the cross is to them that perish foolishness; but unto us which are saved it is the power of God" (1 Corinthians 1:18)

Apostle Paul writes that the message of the cross of Christ is foolishness to those, who are perishing, but to those who are saved it is the power of God.

Paul preached the Gospel of Jesus and his crucifixion, but it was foolishness to Greeks. But the message of cross is power for those who believe in Jesus.

"For by one Spirit are we all baptized into one body, whether we be Jews or Gentiles, whether we be bond or free; and have been all made to drink into one Spirit". (1 Corinthians 12:13)

When Paul came to know that there were contentions and divisions among the followers of Christ, and some of them identified themselves as belonging to Apollos, and some to Cephas, and some to Christ, he questioned them if Christ was divided? He further questioned them if he himself was crucified for them.

To the Jews the message of cross was not acceptable because they did not believe that Jesus bore our sins on the cross; rather they wanted to see signs and proofs.

To the Greeks, who believed in philosophy and wisdom of this world, the message of cross was foolishness. Paul's main motto was to preach the gospel of Jesus. Speaking of Jesus he says...

"Who gave himself for our sins, that he might deliver us from this present evil world, according to the will of God and our Father" (Galatians 1:4)

Paul laid emphasis on preaching 'Christ crucified' rather than usage of clever and attractive words, luring men into false confidence, and false promises of good health, or enough wealth, or guaranteed prosperous life.

Any other type of preaching without showing the truth of the cross where the Son of God shed his precious blood will be of no effect. Temporary assuage may be achieved by preaching resting on false promises, but sooner or later such preaching would be denounced.

God destroys the wise men of this world that treat the message of cross with contempt. Everything in this world is transient and temporary. What lasts is the eternal life that can be had only by faith in Jesus, who has paid price for our salvation. It is the gift of God and cannot be purchased with any amount of wealth of this world. (cf. 1 Corinthians 1:17-23)

The believers of this grace period, irrespective of Jews or Gentiles, who will caught up to meet the Lord in the air, and the dead who shall rise including the Old Testament believers, who rise up before the Church is caught up, will be with the Lord always and their residence will be in New Jerusalem that comes down from heaven.

Those Jews who are saved during Great Tribulation period will be with the Lord at his second advent on this earth, when he steps down his feet on the Mount of Olives, there is the new earth, and the Temple at Jerusalem. Jesus rules for thousand years from the throne of David.

This is the difference between the earthly Jerusalem and the New Jerusalem that comes down from heaven.

John saw a new heaven and a new earth after the first heaven and the first earth passed away and there was no more sea.

In this New Jerusalem there was not seen any difference between Jews or Gentiles, but those who were there were all one in Christ.

They had put on righteousness of Christ as their garments. They had received Jesus as their personal Savior and Lord by grace through faith in him.

JESUS SAID "Except a man be born again, he cannot see the kingdom of God"

What does it mean to be born-again?

"Jesus answered and said unto him, Verily, verily, I say unto thee, Except a man be born again, he cannot see the kingdom of God. Nicodemus saith unto him, How can a man be born when he is old? can he enter the second time into his mother's womb, and be born? Jesus answered, Verily, verily,

I say unto thee, Except a man be born of water and of the Spirit, he cannot enter into the kingdom of God". (John 3:3-5)

Jesus Christ died for our sins; he rose from the dead and ascended into heaven. He is now seated at the right hand of the Majesty and He is coming again soon.

HIS ONLY BEGOTTEN SON

"For God so loved the world, that he gave his only begotten Son, that whosoever believeth in him should not perish, but have everlasting life" (John 3:16)

Jesus said: "Therefore doth my Father love me, because I lay down my life, that I might take it again". (John 10:17)

SALVATION IS FREE OF COST

According to Bible good works alone will not get us into heaven but faith in Lord Jesus Christ alone saves us. Confession by mouth and the belief that God raised Him from the dead will get us salvation free of cost.

Salvation is free. No amount of good works can get a person a place in heaven. The works will follow faith in Jesus Christ and salvation. May the Word of God speak to our hearts

CHAPTER 19
INVITATION TO SALVATION

GOD IS A SPIRIT

The answer to an intriguing question as to how does God look like is found in the Gospel according to John Chapter 4 verse 24 which reads..."God is a Spirit: and they that worship him must worship him in spirit and in truth".

Did anyone see God? God sent His only begotten Son into this world that whosoever believes in Him shall not perish but have everlasting life. "For God so loved the world, that he gave his only begotten Son, that whosoever believeth in him should not perish, but have everlasting life". (John 3:16)

The very few verses from John's Gospel 1st Chapter present to us great Truth that "In the beginning was the Word, and the Word was with God, and the Word was God.

The same was in the beginning with God. All things were made by him; and without him was not anything made that was made. In him was life;

and the life was the light of men". (John 1:1-4). The word became flesh.

It is so amazing that the Almighty God who created heaven and who cannot be contained in man-made buildings loved man so much that He sent His only begotten Son for our sake.

God is a Spirit (John 4:24) and He went before the children of Israel by day in a pillar of a cloud and led them; and he went before them in a pillar of fire by night to give them light. (Exodus 13:21).

The LORD went before the children of Israel in a thick cloud in order that the people may hear when He speaks to Moses. (Exodus 19:9)

The LORD dwelt among them unseen by any one, yet performing miracles and helping them. In the Old Testament period God came and dwelt among the children of Israel and in the New Testament period the incarnate God humbled himself and dwelt among men in the form of man.

"And the LORD descended in the cloud, and stood with him there, and proclaimed the name of the LORD". (Exodus 34:5)

"And the Word was made flesh, and dwelt among us, (and we beheld his glory, the glory as of the only begotten of the Father,) full of grace and truth". (John 1:14)

"Who, being in the form of God, thought it not robbery to be equal with God: But made himself of no reputation, and took upon him the form of a servant, and was made in the likeness of men: And being found in fashion as a man, he humbled himself, and became obedient unto death, even the death of the cross " (Philippians 2:6-8)

HAS ANYONE SEEN GOD?

"No man hath seen God at any time; the only begotten Son, which is in the bosom of the Father, he hath declared him" (John 1:18)

JESUS WAS BORN AS MAN

"For unto us a child is born, unto us a son is given: and the government shall be upon his shoulder: and his name shall be called Wonderful, Counsellor, The mighty God, The everlasting Father, The Prince of Peace" Isaiah 9:6

Seven hundred years before Christ, there lived a prophet called Isaiah. Isaiah 9:6 was a prophecy about Lord Jesus Christ.

Once upon a time there was a man sitting in the porch of his home watching birds at a distance. He threw some grains near him and waited to see if birds would come near to him.

Birds slowly hopped, jumped and came near but not so near as to reach the grains because they feared if they came too near the man would harm them.

The man realized that the birds were afraid and were, therefore, not coming near to him. The man, therefore, took the form of bird, and flew into their midst. The birds were happy and followed him to the grains and ate them. That was just a story.

When it comes to man he sinned and went far from God, who sent His only begotten Son, in the likeness of man to reconcile men unto the Father. The 'Son of God' became the 'Son of Man'.

In New Testament, Luke Chapter 1 verses 26 to 38 we read, "God sent the angel Gabriel to Nazareth, a town of Galilee, to a virgin pledged to be married to a man named Joseph, a descendent of David. The virgin's name was Mary.

The angel went to her and said, "Greetings, you who are highly favored! The Lord is with you."

When Mary was afraid, the angel said, "Do not be afraid, Mary you have found favor with God. You will be with child and give birth to a son, and you are to give him the name Jesus. He will be great and will be called the Son of the Most High.

The Lord will give him the throne of David, and he will reign over the house of Jacob forever, his kingdom will never end. "How this will be," Mary asked the angel, "since I am a virgin?" The angel answered, "The Holy Spirit will come upon you, and the power of the Most High will overshadow you. So the holy one to be born will be called the Son of God."

Before Joseph and Mary came together, Mary was found with child through Holy Spirit. Because Joseph was a righteous man and did not want to expose her to public disgrace, he had in mind to put her away quietly.

Angel of the Lord appeared to Joseph in a dream and said, "Joseph son of David, do not be afraid to take Mary home as your wife, because what is conceived in her is from the Holy Spirit.

She will give birth to a son, and you are to give him the name Jesus, because he will save his people from their sins" (cf. Mt.1:18-24).

JESUS WAS FULLY DIVINE AND FULLY HUMAN

Prophet Isaiah's words were fulfilled. When Joseph woke up, he did what the angel of the Lord had commanded him and took Mary home as his wife. But he had no union with her until she gave birth to a son.

Jesus was born in a manger in Bethlehem. He grew up in a poor family, preached the Kingdom of God, Way to obtain salvation, died for our sake upon the cross of Calvary, was buried and rose upon the third day. Later, he ascended in to heaven

Jesus was called the "Son of Man". Jesus was fully divine and fully human when He was on this earth.

His name was Jesus. He is Lord of all and He is the Christ, the Savior.

"God is not a man, that he should lie; neither the son of man, that he should repent: hath he said, and shall he not do [it]? or hath he spoken, and shall he not make it good?" Numbers 23:19

"But Jesus held his peace. And the high priest answered and said unto him, I adjure thee by the living God, that thou tell us whether thou be the Christ, the Son of God. Jesus saith unto him, Thou hast said: nevertheless I say unto you, Hereafter shall ye see the Son of man sitting on the right hand of power, and coming in the clouds of heaven" Matthew 26:63,64

Salvation belongs to Him and Him alone and there is no salvation in any other.

"And Simon Peter answered and said, Thou art the Christ, the Son of the living God." Matthew 16:16

In the days when Lord Jesus was on this earth the people saw God in Jesus and yet did not know that He was God. He was fully divine and fully human.

Jesus grew up and taught the way to the Father. He said "I am the way, the truth, and the life: no man cometh unto the Father, but by me". He also said "If ye had known me, ye should have known my Father also: and from henceforth ye know him, and have seen him".

Then, Philip said to Lord Jesus to show the Father and Jesus said to him "Have I been so long time with you, and yet hast thou not known me, Philip? he that hath seen me hath seen the Father; and how sayest thou then, Shew us the Father?"

Lord Jesus was God in human form. He did miracles like giving sight to the blind, raising the dead. He said to them to believe that He was in the Father and Father in Him. (Cf. John 14:6-11)

Jesus was to die and before He died on the cross he said to the disciples that He will not leave them comfortless.

He said that He would send the Comforter, who was the Holy Spirit, whom the Father would send in His name and that Holy Spirit would teach them as also all of us all things and bring all things into remembrance. In our days we have

Holy Spirit with us and in those who are born again. (Cf. John 14:18-21 and25-27)

MOSES DESIRED TO SEE GOD

"And Moses said unto the LORD, See, thou sayest unto me, Bring up this people: and thou hast not let me know whom thou wilt send with me. Yet thou hast said, I know thee by name, and thou hast also found grace in my sight" (Exodus 33:12)

Moses finds a reason to plead with God and expresses his desire to see Him. The reason he quoted was that God said to him that He asked him to lead the people of Israel but did not tell him who will accompany him and yet he said that He knew Moses' name.

Moses desired to see God and prayed to Him to show Himself that Moses may know God fully well and know that Israel is His nation and the children of Israel are His people.

"Now therefore, I pray thee, if I have found grace in thy sight, shew me now thy way, that I may know thee, that I may find grace in thy sight: and consider that this nation is thy people" (Exodus 33:13)

God said to Moses that he found grace in the sight of Him and He knew Moses by his name. God said that He will make His goodness pass before Moses and will be gracious to him and show mercy on those whom He will have mercy. God also said to Moses that he cannot see God's face because no man can see God and live after seeing His face.

God provided a solution to Moses that he should stand at a designated place upon a rock and when the glory of God passes by He shall place Moses in a cleft of the rock and cover him with His hand while He passes by. After God passing by the place He would lift His hand and Moses could see His back parts but face shall not be seen (Exodus 33:17-23)

God had given to Moses two tablets containing the Ten Commandments as we read in Exodus Chapter 20 but then when he went down from the mount with the two tablets of the testimony, the work of God and the writing of God, in his hand he saw calf and the dancing. Moses' anger waxed hot and he cast the tables out of his hand and broke them. (cf. Exodus 32:15-19).

Moses saw God as detailed in Exodus 33:17-23 the LORD said to Moses to hew two tablets of stone like the first one "and the LORD descended in the cloud and stood with him there and proclaimed the name of the LORD" (Exodus 34:5)

Moses worshipped God and prayed that the LORD may go among the children of Israel. The LORD made covenant that He will drive out the Amorites, the Canaanites, the Hittites, Perizzites, the Hivite and the Jebusite.

Moses did not see God face to face because God is a Spirit and He had no physical body and God Himself said no one can see Him in His glory and live. Moses could hear the voice of the LORD.

HOW DID GOD SPEAK TO MAN?

"God, who at sundry times and in divers manners spake in time past unto the fathers by the prophets, Hath in these last days spoken unto us by his Son, whom he hath appointed heir of all things, by whom also he made the worlds; Who being the brightness of his glory, and the express image of his person, and upholding all things by the word of his power, when he had by himself purged our sins, sat down on the right hand of the Majesty on high" (Hebrews 1:1-3)

God spoke to Adam, Abraham, Moses and many other prophets in the Old Testament period and to many in the New Testament period and to many after His resurrection and ascension.

From Genesis account it is clear that God had a perfect relationship with Adam and He walked in the cool of the day in the Garden of Eden. Adam transgressed the commandment of God and hid himself when God inquired of him as to where he was.

Adam said he was naked, and, therefore, he hid from God. Adam knew that he was naked only after he transgressed the commandment of God. God covered Adam with the skin of a dead animal by removing the apron he made for himself with the leaves by his own works. His works to cover his nakedness was not enough in the sight of God and He made His own provision for covering the nakedness of Adam.

During this period much conversation took place between God and Adam. God expelled Adam and

Eve from the Garden of Eden in order that he may not lay hands on the tree of life.

Man fell from the presence of God and man's posterity could not see the glory of God from then onwards until Lord Jesus Christ, who was with Father, came into this world in the form of servant in the likeness of man to redeem him from the bondage of sin provided he repented of his sin and to reconcile man with the Father.

God spoke to Moses from the burning bush.

"And when the LORD saw that he turned aside to see, God called unto him out of the midst of the bush, and said, Moses, Moses. And he said, Here am I" Exodus 3:4

God spoke to Moses, His servant and Aaron, the high priest from "Mercy Seat" in the Tabernacle. God spoke to Abraham by coming in the form of man. God spoke to prophets through visions and in dreams. Lord Jesus was present with Shadrach, Meshach, and Abednego in fiery furnace (Christophany).

GOD SPOKE IN DIFFERENT WAYS

"And after the earthquake a fire; [but] the LORD [was] not in the fire: and after the fire a still small voice" 1 Kings 19:12

During the journey of Israelites in the wilderness God spoke to Moses several times. One such incidence is found in Exodus 19:16-19.

There were thunders and lightening and a thick cloud upon the Mount Sinai The trumpet sound was exceedingly loud and the people trembled.

While the people waited near the Mount Sinai God descended upon it in fire and some ascended as the smoke from a furnace. Mount Sinai was on a smoke and God responded to Moses in a voice.

In 1 Kings 18:20-40 there is a dramatic presentation of how Elijah proved that Jehovah is the real God, the God of heaven and earth, the God who created heavens, earth, seas and all that is therein.

Baal and four hundred and fifty prophets of Baal were humiliated and Elijah killed them all. The idol remained an idol speechless. God showed up on

Mount Carmel in the form of fire and consumed the burnt sacrifice offered by Elijah.

Elijah was afraid of the threatening made by Jezebel, wife of wicked king, Ahab. She threatened to kill Elijah, and somehow Elijah's fear exceeded the success he had seen earlier. He went and hid in a cave where an angel of the Lord appeared to him and asked him to be courageous, rise and eat.

Elijah obeyed and rose and ate for forty days and forty nights on the mount.

The LORD said to Elijah to stand upon the mount and Elijah did as the LORD said to him. God passed by and behold there was great and strong wind rent the mountains and broke the rocks but He was not there.

After this an earthquake took place and after earthquake a fire, but the LORD was not in the fire, but after the fire there God came to Elijah in a small still voice and spoke to him.

The word of the LORD came to Elijah and asked him "What doest thou here, Elijah?" Prophet Elijah answered the LORD God of hosts that he was very jealous for the LORD and while the children of Israel forsook the covenant, he was all alone left to stand for the LORD and his life is being sought after. God said to Elijah that there were He reserved seven thousand in Israel who did not bow their knees to Baal.

"Yet I have left [me] seven thousand in Israel, all the knees which have not bowed unto Baal, and every mouth which hath not kissed him" 1 Kings 19:18

In the following references we see that God spoke in fire, thunder, whirlwind besides speaking in still small voice.

Job 37:2 "Hear attentively the noise of his voice, and the sound [that] goeth out of his mouth"

Job 38:1 "Then the LORD answered Job out of the whirlwind, and said"

Psalm 104:7 "At thy rebuke they fled; at the voice of thy thunder they hasted away.

Zechariah 4:6 Then he answered and spake unto me, saying, This [is] the word of the LORD unto Zerubbabel, saying, Not by might, nor by power, but by my spirit, saith the LORD of hosts" John 12:29 "The people therefore, that stood by, and heard [it], said that it thundered: others said, An angel spake to him" Revelation 4:5 "And out of the throne proceeded lightnings and thunderings and voices: and [there were] seven lamps of fire burning before the throne, which are the seven Spirits of God"

Thus we see that God spoke to man in different ways in different periods and the writer of Hebrews rightly said:

"God, who at sundry times and in divers manners spake in time past unto the fathers by the prophets, Hath in these last days spoken unto us by [his] Son, whom he hath appointed heir of all things, by whom also he made the worlds" Hebrews 1:1-2

GOD SPOKE BY HIS SON

"Hath in these last days spoken unto us by [his] Son, whom he hath appointed heir of all things, by whom also he made the worlds" Hebrews 1:2

Lord Jesus Christ spoke about the Father and said He and the Father are one and whoever has seen

Him has seen the Father. The Son of God, Lord Jesus Christ, relinquished His glory in heaven, and came into this world. The Father, The Son, and The Holy Spirit are one and co-equal and co-existence. Lord Jesus Christ is the way, the truth and the life.

"I and my Father are one." John 10:30

"No man can come to me, except the Father which hath sent me draw him: and I will raise him up at the last day" John 6:44

"For he hath made him [to be] sin for us, who knew no sin; that we might be made the righteousness of God in him" 2 Corinthians 5:21

Lord Jesus Christ, the Son of God, became mediator between the Father and man to give man salvation. Lord Jesus Christ paid the price of redemption of man by taking upon Him the sin of man and dying on the cross. His blood cleanses us from our sin provided we repent of our sins.

In the New Testament period before Jesus ascended into heaven he spoke in person face to face to some.

"Jesus saith unto her, Woman, why weepest thou? whom seekest thou? She, supposing him to be the gardener, saith unto him, Sir, if thou have borne him hence, tell me where thou hast laid him, and I will take him away" John 20:15

After Lord Jesus Christ is seated at the right hand of the Majesty Holy Spirit came into this world to be with His disciples and with all those who believed Him as Savior. The Holy Spirit dwelt in the believers as soon as they accepted Jesus as their Savior.

In the present age God speaks to us from His Holy Word and the Spirit who speaks strongly to us in our hearts convicting us the truth and providing way to escape from sinning.

God also speaks through preachers, teachers of the Word of God and sometimes also from the mouths of our closed ones, if they were believers in Lord Jesus Christ and had salvation.

In the kingdom age when Lord Jesus Christ comes He will speak to those who were justified as righteous during "Great Tribulation Period" and justified as righteous in the "Sheep and Goat judgment"

in the same way as He spoke to His disciples and others after His resurrection from the dead. Every eye will see Lord Jesus Christ and acknowledge that He is Lord Jesus Christ, the Son of God, and the Savior.

"Behold, he cometh with clouds; and every eye shall see him, and they also which pierced him: and all kindreds of the earth shall wail because of him. Even so, Amen"(Revelation 1:7)

Today is the day of Salvation. It is your choice. Jesus Christ, who bore our sins and died for our sake, is resurrected and He is living God. He will come soon to receive the saved ones to be with Him eternally.

Please do not lose this opportunity but confess your sins to him and be saved. It is not a way to convert you Christianity. God has his own ways of gaining men for himself.

My message is a request that you may please accept Jesus Christ as your personal Savior, and as

your Lord, so that you may have everlasting life
just as I have gained peace through Him.

www.ingramcontent.com/pod-product-compliance
Lightning Source LLC
Chambersburg PA
CBHW060512030426
42337CB00015B/1867